Sensei Self Development

Mental Health Chronicles Series

Exploring Your Values and Making Decisions

Sensei Paul David

Copyright Page

Sensei Self Development -
Exploring Your Values and Making Decisions,
by Sensei Paul David

Copyright © 2024

All rights reserved.

978-1-77848-345-5
SSD_Journals_Amazon_PaperbackBook_ Exploring Your Values and Making Decisions

978-1-77848-344-8 SSD_Journals_Amazon_eBook_ Exploring Your Values and Making Decisions

978-1-77848-459-9
SSD_Journals_Ingram_Paperback_Exploring Your Values and Making Decisions

This book is not authorized for free distribution copying.

www.senseipublishing.com

@senseipublishing
#senseipublishing

Get/Share Your FREE SSD Mental Health Chronicles at
www.senseiselfdevelopment.care

or

CLICK HERE

Check Out The SSD Chronicles Series CLICK HERE

Dedication

To those who courageously take action towards self-improvement - you are helping to evolve the world for generations to come.

- It's a great day to be alive!

If Found Please Contact:

_____

Reward If Found:

_____

MY COMMITMENT

I, _____ commit to writing This Sensei Self Development Journal for at least 10 days in a row, starting: _____

Writing this journal is valuable to me because:

_____
_____
_____
_____
_____
_____

If I finish a minimum of 10 consecutive days of writing in this journal, I will reward myself by:

_____
_____
_____
_____

_____

_____

If I don't finish 10 days of writing this journal, I will promise to:

_____

_____

_____

_____

_____

I will do the following things to ensure that I write in my Sensei Self Development Journal every day:

_____

_____

_____

_____

_____

Get/Share Your FREE All-Ages Mental Health eBook Now at
www.senseiselfdevelopment.com
Or CLICK HERE

senseiselfdevelopment.com

Check Out Another Book In The SSD BOOK SERIES:
senseipublishing.com/SSD_SERIES
CLICK HERE

Join Our Publishing Journey!

If you would like to receive FUTURE FREE BOOKS and get to know us better, please click www.senseipublishing.com and join our newsletter by entering your email address in the pop-up box.

Follow Our Blog: senseipauldavid.ca

Follow/Like/Subscribe: Facebook, Instagram, YouTube: @senseipublishing

Scan the QR Code with your phone or tablet
to follow us on social media: Like / Subscribe / Follow

A Message From The Author:
Sensei Paul David

Dear Reader,

Welcome to the world of mental health journaling – a sacred space for self-reflection, growth, and healing. Within these pages, you hold the power to uplift your spirit, invigorate your mind, and nourish your goals.

In a world that often moves at blink-and-you'll-miss-it speed, it's crucial to make time for self-care and self-discovery.

Anxiety, stress, and emotional turbulence may have clouded your mind, making it difficult to find clarity and peace within. But fear not! Together, we will navigate the labyrinth of emotions, and experiences, helping to simplify the path to mental well-being.

This journal is not merely a bunch of blank pages awaiting your words. It is your compassionate companion, offering solace and understanding during your unique journey. Here, you are free to unburden yourself, celebrate small and large victories, and confront the challenges that may still linger.

Within the sheltered realm of these pages, there is no judgment, no expectation, and no pressure. Your unique experience and perspective hold immeasurable worth, and your voice deserves to be heard. Whether you choose to fill the lines with eloquence or simply scribble fragments of your thoughts, please remember each entry is a valuable contribution to your growth.

In this sacred space, you are challenged to take off the mask we so often wear in the outside world. It is here that you can be raw, vulnerable, and authentic – allowing your true self to be seen and embraced without reservation. By giving yourself permission to explore the depths of your emotions and confront the shadows that may lurk within, you will discover profound insights and find the healing you seek over time.

As you embark on this journaling journey, I encourage you to embrace the process itself rather than fixate solely on the outcome. Remember, it is not about reaching a certain destination or ticking off boxes on a list of accomplishments. Rather, it is about cultivating self-awareness, fostering self-compassion, and nurturing a sense of curiosity about the intricate workings of your intelligently beautiful mind.

In the quiet moments of reflection, let your pen become a bridge between your inner world and the possibilities that lie ahead. Create a sanctuary for your thoughts, fears, triumphs, and dreams. As you pour your heart onto these pages, allow your words to be a living testament to courage, resilience, and an unwavering commitment to your own well-being.

I am honored to be a part of your journey, and I believe in your ability to navigate the twists and turns with grace and resilience. Remember, you are not alone in this – countless others have walked similar paths, faced similar challenges, and emerged stronger and wiser on the other side. You have the power to reclaim all of your untapped joy, cultivate a positive mindset that serves you, and foster a deep sense of self-love and peaceful confident. – And it will take a worth effort and time.

So, open the first page of this journal with hope, curiosity, and an open heart and open mind. Embrace the transformative power of self-reflection, and allow it to guide you towards a life of greater fulfilment and peace. Each journaling session is an opportunity to not only connect with yourself but also to rekindle the light within that sometimes flickers but never extinguishes.

Remember, the pages you are about to fill are not just a record of your journey but also a testament to your strength, resilience, and indomitable spirit. Cherish this space, invest in yourself, and let your words be an ode to the magnificent journey of becoming whole.

With great respect for your decision to evolve,

Paul

MY CONVICTION

Please circle your answers below

I am DECIDING to be patient with myself and this PROCESS each time I journal toward my improved state of mental well-being

YES   NO

"The present moment is filled with joy and happiness. If you are attentive, you will see it."

Thich Nhat Hanh

Introduction

In 1838, Charles Darwin, on the brink of turning 30, was grappling with a decision: whether to get married and potentially have children. To sort through his thoughts, Darwin made a list. On one side, he listed the positives of marriage, imagining a life with a "constant companion," someone to love and cherish, even thinking it would be better than having a dog. On the other side, he considered the benefits of remaining single, like the freedom from obligatory visits to relatives and the ease of not having to compromise over every small matter.

Darwin was facing what could be called a 'wild problem' - a life-altering decision where the right choice is not immediately clear, where the day-to-day benefits and drawbacks of each option are hidden, and where these daily experiences don't fully capture the significance of the choice.

We often encounter just a few major decisions like this in life - deciding whether to marry, who to marry, if we should have children, or whether to change careers and take on new roles. Usually, there's not much information to help us make these choices, and the little information we do have can sometimes lead us astray. So, how do we move forward, particularly if we're aiming to make a well-thought-out, rational decision?

For centuries, philosophers have delved into how we make choices, trying to figure out what makes a decision good or bad, logical or illogical. They've mostly agreed on a concept called "Decision theory," which suggests that good decisions are based on our values. For instance, if you're choosing between majoring in economics or art history, you start by considering what you value most, then aim to maximize that value.

This approach treats a decision like a formula where you weigh your values. Imagine you're deciding whether to bring an umbrella when you go out. You might use a formula that considers the likelihood of rain, the joy of walking freely, and the annoyance of getting wet. While this example is simple, decision theory suggests that there's a formula for everything, whether it's a complex military operation or drilling for oil in the North Sea. You input your values, and the theory helps determine the best choice.

imagine you're trying to decide where to go on vacation. You might care about several things: relaxation, adventure, experiencing new cultures, or keeping costs low. Using decision theory, you'd give each of these factors a 'weight' based on how important they are to you.

Say you love relaxing more than anything. A quiet beach might score high on your list. But if you're all about exploring and culture, a bustling city with lots of history could be your top pick.

You'd look at each option and evaluate how well they match up with your values - like how relaxing a beach is, how exciting a city tour might be, how enriching a historical landmark visit could be, or how affordable each choice is. Then, you pick the one that best aligns with what's most important to you.

How to Make Good Decisions

Good decision-making is really about two main things:

1. Learning how to get what you want.
2. Figuring out what is actually worth wanting.

The first point is about making choices that work, that get you results. The second is about making choices that are actually good for you in the long run. They might sound the same, but there's a big difference.

Think of it like this: a decision that quickly gets you what you want, like making a sale or hiring someone fast, is effective. But it might not lead to what's really important, like lasting relationships, happiness, or health. Good decisions are those that match up with your bigger life goals and what you really value, and they bring you true satisfaction in your career, with your friends and family, and in your personal life.

Effective decisions give you quick wins, but good decisions lead to real, lasting success.

It all comes down to this: good decisions are always effective in the long run, but not all quick wins are truly good for you. The best choices are those that get you what you really want in life, not just what you think you want right now.

In our lives, we often regret both the things we've done and the things we haven't. But the deepest regret comes from not living a life that's true to ourselves, from not following our own path and values.

Several common patterns can set us up for this kind of regret. First, there's the social pattern where we adopt goals based on other people's expectations, ignoring how different our lives and needs might be from theirs. Then there's the inertia pattern, where we keep chasing old goals even after realizing they don't bring us happiness. The emotional pattern can lead us astray too, making us chase fleeting desires at the cost of our long-term aspirations. And finally, the ego pattern often drives us to seek wealth, status, and power, sometimes sacrificing our happiness and the well-being of others in the process.

If you let these patterns dictate your life, you're likely heading towards regret. Don't live by someone else's standards or let others set your life's goals. It's crucial to take charge of your own journey, to decide where you are now and where you want to go.

Discovering Your Values

Step 1: Find Your Values

Your values aren't hidden; they are reflections of what matters most in your life. To bring these values into focus, try the following:

1) Reflect on your priorities.

"Values" are just a term for the things that are most important to you. Ask yourself: What do I value most in life? Write down as many things as you can think of. Your list should represent what truly matters to you, not what you think should matter based on others' opinions (like those of family, friends, or society).

Honesty is key in this step. Aim to condense your thoughts into a few words (you'll delve deeper and define these values more clearly later on). Examples of values could be family, money, comfort, friends, career, time, freedom, optimism. Remember, these should be things that genuinely resonate with you.

2) Pick Your Top Three Values

You might feel like all the values you listed are important, and they likely are. However, some values will stand out as being more crucial to you than others. Be honest with yourself during this process. If choosing three is tough, it's okay to pick two or four. The goal is to keep your list concise.

3) Rank them

After selecting your top values, consider whether they hold equal weight for you or if you can rank them. There's no right or wrong way to do this. The way you prioritize them will shed light on their significance in your life.

Remember, identifying your values is not a one-off task. It may take weeks or even months to finalize your top values. Be patient and open to revisiting and adjusting your list. When I did this exercise, it took almost a year to solidify my values. Initially, I recognized "happiness" and "fairness" as key values. Only later did I add "freedom," a value so intrinsic to me that I hadn't identified it at first. Be aware that new values might emerge or become more important over time.

Step 2: Define Your Values

Now that you've identified your values, it's time to define them in your own words. Don't rely on dictionary definitions; your personal interpretation is what matters here.

For instance, take the value of "freedom." I define it as the ability to do whatever I want, whenever I want, in any way I choose. This includes both big-picture freedom, like travel, and everyday freedoms, like mental independence. Conversely, one of my clients defines freedom as having the autonomy to make decisions and act without being micromanaged. Same value, but our definitions are distinctly different.

Initially, you might feel like writing lengthy explanations for each value. However, aim for brevity in your definitions – a short, memorable sentence for each value is ideal. This way, you can easily recall what each value means to you. A good test is to ask yourself: If someone woke me up in the middle of the night and asked about my values, could I clearly define them?

As you go about defining your values, remember not to get overwhelmed by the general nature of the words, and don't let others sway your interpretation. For instance, when I say "happiness" is a key value for me, some might dismiss it as too vague or generic. However, for me, "happiness" has a very specific meaning: it's about finding joy in the process of whatever I'm doing.

The words might be broad, but it's important to give them precise and personal definitions that resonate with you. Your interpretation is what gives these values depth and makes them genuinely yours.

How to Make Decisions Based on Values

In recent years, a growing field that combines insights from cognitive science, management theory, and literary studies has developed a variety of tools to aid in better decision-making. When you're faced with a complex choice, one that requires deep thought and whose impact could last years or even decades, you have more options than just a simple pro-and-con list like Darwin's.

These modern tools aren't straightforward solutions; think of them more as prompts, tricks, or rules of thumb, known as heuristics by cognitive scientists. They're designed to help you view your situation from different angles, explore new possibilities, and consider your choices with greater insight and understanding. There's no perfect formula for making tough life decisions. However, research indicates that these tools can improve your decision-making skills.

One significant insight from decision-making research is the importance of exploring different options. In the 1980s, Professor Paul Nutt set out to study decision-making in the real world. He looked at decisions made by top managers in various organizations in the U.S. and Canada, like insurance companies, government bodies, hospitals, and consulting firms.

His research, which began with a study published in 1984, had an eye-opening finding: Only about 15% of these decisions involved looking for new options beyond the initial ones considered. In a later study, he found that less than a third of decision-makers thought about more than one alternative.

This approach, Nutt found, isn't the best. Over the years, his and other researchers' work showed a clear connection between considering multiple alternatives and making successful decisions. In one study, Nutt found that when decision-makers only looked at one option, they viewed their decision as a failure more than half the time. But when they considered at least two options, they saw their decision as a success two-thirds of the time. This shows the value of not rushing to a decision and instead taking the time to explore different possibilities.

The main idea is simple: If you're facing a decision that seems like a straightforward "yes or no" choice, it's better to reframe it as a "which one" question. This opens up more options to consider.

Once you have these options, how should you evaluate them? One technique is called scenario planning. Developed in the 1970s by some management consultants, it involves imagining three different future scenarios for each option: one where things improve, one where they get worse, and one that's completely unexpected.

We all naturally think in stories when making big decisions. For example, if you're thinking of moving to the suburbs, you might imagine a life with family hikes, good schools, and a garden. But formal scenario planning goes further by deeply analyzing these stories and creating multiple ones. What if your children don't settle in well, or part of your family misses the city? This approach encourages you to consider a variety of potential outcomes, not just the first or most positive one that comes to mind.

Psychologist Gary Klein has created an interesting variation of scenario planning known as a "premortem." This technique is inspired by the medical procedure of a post-mortem analysis but with a key twist. In a post-mortem, the subject has already passed away, and the examiner's job is to determine the cause of death. However, in a premortem, the process is reversed.

In a premortem, as explained by Dr. Klein, planners are asked to imagine that it's months into the future and their plan has been implemented. But instead of succeeding, it has failed. They don't know the details of why or how; they just know that the plan didn't work out. Their task is to figure out potential reasons for this failure. So, essentially they are asked to anticipate the problems.

This approach encourages people to identify and analyze potential problems before they occur, allowing them to address weaknesses in their plans proactively. It's a useful technique for thorough planning and risk assessment.

In Dr. Klein's experience, the premortem technique is significantly more effective in identifying the potential weaknesses of a decision. Common cognitive biases like groupthink and confirmation bias can often obscure the pitfalls of a decision once we've committed to it. Just asking ourselves, "What could be wrong with this plan?" isn't usually enough, as we might already be too invested in the decision to see it objectively.

The premortem approach circumvents these issues. By forcing us to assume that the decision has already led to a disaster, it encourages us to think critically about where things might go wrong. This perspective helps to uncover blind spots and challenge the false sense of confidence that can come with initial plans.

Once you have gone through these steps, you'll eventually reach a point where you have to make a decision. Sometimes, the earlier phases of decision-making lead to an obvious best choice. But if you're still facing a tough decision, the final phase can be aided by what's known as a value model. This tool is a more sophisticated and effective version of the classic pros and cons list.

To use a value model in decision-making, you start by listing the values most important to you. For example, when Darwin was deciding whether to marry, his values included freedom, companionship, engaging in clever conversations at clubs, and having children. Once you have your list, the next step is to assign a "weight" to each value, reflecting its importance to you. In a more mathematical approach, you assign a weight between 0 and 1 to each value. For instance, if engaging in clever conversations isn't very important to you, you might assign it a weight of 0.25, whereas the desire to have children, if it's highly important, might be assigned a weight of 0.90.

With your values and their weights established, you then evaluate each option in relation to these values. You grade how well each option satisfies each of your core values on a scale from 1 to 100. For Darwin, remaining a bachelor might score low on the value of having children but might score higher in terms of freedom and access to clever conversations.

Once you've graded each option against your values, the next step involves some basic math: Multiply each grade by the weight of its corresponding value, and then sum up these numbers for each scenario. The scenario with the highest total score is considered the best choice.

This method goes beyond the traditional pros and cons list by quantifying your preferences. It forces you to evaluate each option systematically against what matters most to you. However, it's important to recognize the limitations of this approach. A pros and cons list often just captures our existing understanding of a decision, without offering new insights. As economist and Nobel laureate Thomas Schelling pointed out, no matter how thorough our analysis or imaginative our thinking, we can't list what never occurs to us. This highlights the inherent challenge in decision-making: We are limited by the scope of our imagination and understanding at any given time.

When faced with hard choices, we're often required to make imaginative leaps: to uncover new paths and outcomes that weren't initially apparent. This is especially true for complex decisions, as each one is a unique combination of variables and circumstances. The tools and methods like the value model, scenario planning, and premortem analysis aren't about providing direct answers. Instead, they assist us in viewing each decision more clearly and from different perspectives.

These tools encourage us to think beyond our initial understanding and to consider a wider range of possibilities and outcomes. They help us to map out the decision-making landscape more comprehensively, revealing aspects and options we might not have considered initially.

Moment Mori: Using Death to Let Your Values Come to the Forefront

You could leave life right now. Let that determine what you do and say and think. — Marcus Aurelius

In the face of death, what you value becomes clear, and what's irrelevant fades into the background. Hence, you can use thinking about death as a tool to make value-based decisions.

Imagine you're torn between two choices. Thinking about death can sharpen your focus, much like putting on a pair of glasses that corrects your vision. Suddenly, you might notice flaws in one option that you hadn't seen before, or you might realize that both choices are equally valuable in their own ways, making the decision a matter of chance.

Often, contemplating death reveals that we're sweating the small stuff. Decisions like choosing between pizza or hamburgers might cause us stress, but in the context of life's bigger picture, they're really not that significant. Remembering our mortality can help us focus on what's truly important and let go of the minor dilemmas that consume our attention.

So, death can act as a heuristic, a shortcut so to say, to quickly make your decisions based on values. Using death might not be as systemic as the methods we just discussed, but it is quick and therefore good for making everyday decisions.

How to Make Small Decisions

Overthinking is a real thing. It can cause a lot of headaches. We are overwhelmed with choices. Which movies to watch? Which cereal to eat? If you go down into details of each decision you are trying to pick, you would short circuit.

And these decisions are not limited to buying choices. They are also related to whether we should go to the mall or the beach, whether we should take a bicycle or take a walk. Whether we should go home or hang out with friends.

You don't want to be like Hamlet, suffering over what to do and what not to do. You need to be thoughtful yet decisive. The best way to do that is to categorize your decisions by considering how consequential they are, and how reversible they are.

Consequential decisions are those that impact the most important aspects of your life, such as whom you marry, where you live, or which business you start. The more a decision influences what's important to you, either now or in the future, the more significant it is. On the flip side, reversible decisions are those that can be undone later. The difficulty or expense involved in reversing a decision indicates how irreversible it is. For example, eating a chocolate bar is irreversible – once you've eaten it, there's no going back. Similarly, having a child is an irreversible decision.

Conversely, some decisions are easy to reverse, like signing up for a free fourteen-day trial; if you change your mind, it's easy to cancel. These various types of decisions can be plotted on a graph based on their level of consequence and reversibility. Among these, two extremes are particularly noteworthy: decisions that are highly consequential and irreversible, and those that are inconsequential and highly reversible. Highly consequential and irreversible decisions have far-reaching, permanent effects – they're like the first domino in a series, setting off a chain reaction. The cost of a mistake here is high.

On the other hand, decisions that are inconsequential and easily reversible have a low risk. If the outcome isn't to your liking, you can simply reverse it with little cost. The real mistake with these decisions is overthinking and expending too much mental energy. If a decision is easily reversible or not very important, spending more time on gathering information is just wasting resources.

If you've ever shopped for a mattress, you've likely experienced this scenario. You invest hours, maybe even days, researching different mattresses. You pore over reviews, compare prices, and debate whether you need a mattress for hot or cold sleepers. After all this effort, you finally choose one and have it delivered, only to discover it's not as perfect as you hoped. In the end, you return it and go with your second choice. This whole process could have been streamlined by simply checking if the store had a good return policy, quickly picking a mattress, and then moving on. When the risk or cost of making a wrong choice is low, it's better to make decisions quickly and efficiently.

Relying too much on methodical decision-making can be unwise, as it can lead to overthinking simple choices. This idea is often humorously portrayed in media, where intelligent characters make unnecessarily complex decisions. Sheldon Cooper from "The Big Bang Theory" is a prime example. His character frequently engages in overly detailed analysis for simple decisions, leading to comical situations. For instance, there's a scene where Sheldon uses scientific principles and environmental variables to determine the optimal temperature for drinking hot beverages.

Before We Get Started…

Remember, mindfulness journaling is a personal practice, and these questions are meant to guide and inspire you. Feel free to adapt and modify them to suit your needs and preferences. Explore, reflect, and embrace the opportunity to deepen your self-awareness and cultivate a sense of inner peace.

Date ___/___/___ : S M T W Th F S

I feel:
(please circle)

because _____ because _____ because _____ because _____ because _____

Today I Am Grateful For

1. _____
2. _____
3. _____

What could help transform today into a remarkable day?

Reflective Writing
How did you come to identify your core values?

_____
_____
_____
_____
_____
_____
_____
_____

Which of the following is NOT a key benefit of identifying your values?

A) Increased self-awareness
B) More meaningful relationships
C) Better decision-making skills
D) Guaranteed success in life

All Are Correct - Choose The Response You Feel Is Most Important To Remember

Date ___/___/___ : S M T W Th F S

I feel:
(please circle)

😊	😁	😋	😣	😠
because	because	because	because	because
_____	_____	_____	_____	_____

Today I Am Grateful For

1. _____
2. _____
3. _____

What could help transform today into a remarkable day?
_____

Reflective Writing

What were some of the biggest challenges you encountered while exploring your values?

_____
_____
_____
_____
_____
_____
_____
_____

Which of the following best describes a personal value?

A) Something that can change frequently

B) Something that is influenced by others

C) Something that guides your beliefs and behaviors

D) Something that is solely determined by society

All Are Correct - Choose The Response You Feel Is Most Important To Remember

Date ___/___/___ : S M T W Th F S

I feel:
(please circle)

😊 because _____
😁 because _____
😋 because _____
😣 because _____
😠 because _____

Today I Am Grateful For
1. _____
2. _____
3. _____

What could help transform today into a remarkable day?

Reflective Writing
What have you learned about yourself through this process?

_____
_____
_____
_____
_____
_____
_____

Which of the following is NOT a common source of our values?

A) Family and upbringing
B) Religion or spirituality
C) Social media influencers
D) Cultural traditions

All Are Correct - Choose The Response You Feel Is Most Important To Remember

Date ___/___/___ : S M T W Th F S

I feel:
(please circle)

😊 because _____ 😁 because _____ 😌 because _____ 😢 because _____ 😠 because _____

Today I Am Grateful For
1. _____
2. _____
3. _____

What could help transform today into a remarkable day?

Reflective Writing
What do you think was the most important factor in making the decisions you have made?

_____

_____

_____

_____

_____

_____

_____

How do our values influence our decision-making?

A) They provide a clear sense of direction
B) They can create conflicts with others' values
C) They dictate what we prioritize in life
D) All of the above

All Are Correct - Choose The Response You Feel Is Most Important To Remember

Date ___/___/___ : S M T W Th F S

I feel:
(please circle)

because _____ because _____ because _____ because _____ because _____

Today I Am Grateful For

1. _____
2. _____
3. _____

What could help transform today into a remarkable day?

Reflective Writing

How have you been able to maintain consistency between your values and the decisions you have made?

_____
_____
_____
_____
_____
_____
_____

Which of the following is a helpful strategy for exploring your values?

A) Comparing your values to others
B) Ignoring any values that cause discomfort
C) Reflecting on experiences that have shaped your values
D) Adopting values solely based on societal norms

All Are Correct - Choose The Response You Feel Is Most Important To Remember

Date ___/___/___ : S M T W Th F S

I feel:
(please circle)

because _____ because _____ because _____ because _____ because _____

Today I Am Grateful For
1. _____
2. _____
3. _____

What could help transform today into a remarkable day?

Reflective Writing
How has understanding and exploring your values impacted your relationships with others?

_____
_____
_____
_____
_____
_____
_____

Which of the following is a common misconception about values?

A) Values are set in stone and cannot change
B) Everyone has the same values
C) Values only apply to personal beliefs
D) Values have no impact on decision-making

All Are Correct - Choose The Response You Feel Is Most Important To Remember

Date ___/___/___ : S M T W Th F S

I feel:
(please circle)

because _____ because _____ because _____ because _____ because _____

Today I Am Grateful For
1. _____
2. _____
3. _____

What could help transform today into a remarkable day?

Reflective Writing

How have your values helped you to prioritize and manage your time?

_____
_____
_____
_____
_____
_____
_____

How can identifying your values help with decision-making?

A) It provides a clear filter for making choices
B) It eliminates all potential risks or challenges
C) It guarantees a favorable outcome
D) None of the above

All Are Correct - Choose The Response You Feel Is Most Important To Remember

Date ___/___/___ : S M T W Th F S

I feel:
(please circle)

because _____ because _____ because _____ because _____ because _____

Today I Am Grateful For
1. _____
2. _____
3. _____

What could help transform today into a remarkable day?

Reflective Writing
How have you been able to effectively communicate your values to others?

_____
_____
_____
_____
_____
_____
_____

Which of the following is an example of an internal value?

A) Honesty
B) Wealth
C) Success
D) Fashion

All Are Correct - Choose The Response You Feel Is Most Important To Remember

Date ___ / ___ / ___ : S M T W Th F S

I feel:
(please circle)

because _____ because _____ because _____ because _____ because _____

Today I Am Grateful For
1. _____
2. _____
3. _____

What could help transform today into a remarkable day?

Reflective Writing
How have you been able to make decisions that reflect your beliefs?

_____

_____

_____

_____

_____

_____

_____

Which of the following factors can potentially influence our values?

A) Personal experiences
B) Peer pressure
C) Media and societal norms
D) All of the above

All Are Correct - Choose The Response You Feel Is Most Important To Remember

Date ___/___/___ : S M T W Th F S

I feel:
(please circle)

😊 because _____ 😄 because _____ 😋 because _____ 😫 because _____ 😠 because _____

Today I Am Grateful For
1. _____
2. _____
3. _____

What could help transform today into a remarkable day?

Reflective Writing
What strategies have you used to stay true to your values when faced with difficult decisions?

_____
_____
_____
_____
_____
_____
_____

How can conflicting values impact our decision-making?

A) It can lead to indecision or internal conflict
B) It forces us to compromise our values
C) It causes a complete disregard for values
D) None of the above

All Are Correct - Choose The Response You Feel Is Most Important To Remember

Date ___/___/___ : S M T W Th F S

I feel:
(please circle)

because because because because because
_____ _____ _____ _____ _____

Today I Am Grateful For
1. _____
2. _____
3. _____

What could help transform today into a remarkable day?
_____

Reflective Writing
What have been some of the benefits of exploring your values?

_____
_____
_____
_____
_____
_____
_____

Why is it important to regularly reassess our values?

A) Our values can change over time
B) It can help us stay true to our core beliefs
C) It ensures we are making decisions based on outdated values
D) All of the above

All Are Correct - Choose The Response You Feel Is Most Important To Remember

Date ___/___/___ : S M T W Th F S

I feel:
(please circle)

😊 because _____ 😁 because _____ 😋 because _____ 😣 because _____ 😠 because _____

Today I Am Grateful For

1. _____
2. _____
3. _____

What could help transform today into a remarkable day?

Reflective Writing

How has this process helped you to be more mindful and deliberate in your decision making?

_____
_____
_____
_____
_____
_____
_____
_____
_____

Which of the following is NOT a helpful strategy for making decisions based on your values?

A) Seeking advice from others
B) Honoring your emotions and intuition
C) Considering the potential consequences of your decision
D) Ignoring any conflicting values

All Are Correct - Choose The Response You Feel Is Most Important To Remember

Date ___/___/___ : S M T W Th F S

I feel:
(please circle)

🙂 because _____
😄 because _____
😊 because _____
😟 because _____
😠 because _____

Today I Am Grateful For
1. _____
2. _____
3. _____

What could help transform today into a remarkable day?

Reflective Writing
How has understanding and exploring your values helped you to make more informed decisions?

_____
_____
_____
_____
_____
_____
_____
_____

How can identifying your values help with setting goals and priorities?

A) It provides clarity and direction
B) It eliminates any potential obstacles or challenges
C) It guarantees success in achieving our goals
D) None of the above

All Are Correct - Choose The Response You Feel Is Most Important To Remember

Date ___/___/___ : S M T W Th F S

I feel:
(please circle)

because because because because because
_____ _____ _____ _____ _____

Today I Am Grateful For

1. _____
2. _____
3. _____

What could help transform today into a remarkable day?

Reflective Writing

What have you learned about yourself through this process that you didn't know before?

_____

_____

_____

_____

_____

_____

_____

Which of the following is an example of an external value?

A) Compassion
B) Physical appearance
C) Independence
D) Curiosity

All Are Correct - Choose The Response You Feel Is Most Important To Remember

Date ___/___/___ : S M T W Th F S

I feel: (please circle)

😊 because _____ 😁 because _____ 😋 because _____ 😣 because _____ 😠 because _____

Today I Am Grateful For
1. _____
2. _____
3. _____

What could help transform today into a remarkable day?

Reflective Writing

How have you been able to maintain consistency between your values and the decisions you have made?

_____
_____
_____
_____
_____
_____
_____

What can we do if our values conflict with societal or cultural norms?

A) Change our values to fit in
B) Ignore our values and conform to societal expectations
C) Align our actions with our values and potentially challenge societal norms
D) None of the above

All Are Correct - Choose The Response You Feel Is Most Important To Remember

As we reach the final pages of this journey through "Positive Mindset," I want to extend my heartfelt thanks to you. Your commitment to exploring positivity and its transformative power is not only commendable but a testament to your desire for personal growth and a richer, more fulfilling life experience.

Remember, the journey towards a positive mindset is ongoing and ever-evolving. Each day presents new opportunities to apply these principles, to learn, and to grow. I encourage you to revisit these pages whenever you need a reminder of your incredible potential to foster positivity and resilience in the face of life's challenges.

As we part ways, I leave you with a quote that has been a guiding star in my journey: "The greatest discovery of any generation is that a human can alter his life by altering his attitude."

– William James.

Thank you for allowing me to be a part of your journey. May your path be filled with light, hope, and endless possibilities. Farewell, and may you carry the spirit of positivity with you, today and always.

With gratitude and best wishes,

Sensei Paul David

Reflective Writing

The End

As you close the pages of this mindfulness journal, remember that each word you've written is a step on your journey towards self-awareness and inner peace. Embrace the moments of clarity, the revelations, and even the uncertainties you've encountered along the way. Let this journal be a testament to your growth and a reminder that every day offers a new opportunity to be present, to observe, and to appreciate the simple wonders of life. Carry these lessons forward, and may your path be filled with mindful moments and serene reflections. Until we meet again in these pages, be gentle with yourself and stay anchored in the now.

Mindfulness isn't difficult, we just need to remember to do it.

Thank You!

If you found this book helpful, I would be grateful if you would **post an honest review on Amazon** so this book can reach other supportive readers like you!

All you need to do is digitally flip to the back and leave your review. Or visit amazon.com/author/senseipauldavid click the correct book cover and click on the blue link next to the yellow stars that say, "customer reviews."

As always...
It's a great day to be alive!

Get/Share Your FREE SSD Mental Health Chronicles at
www.senseiselfdevelopment.care

Check Out The SSD Chronicles Series CLICK HERE

Get/Share Your FREE All-Ages Mental Health eBook Now at
www.senseiselfdevelopment.com
Or CLICK HERE

senseiselfdevelopment.com

Click Another Book In The SSD BOOK SERIES:
senseipublishing.com/SSD_SERIES
CLICK HERE

Join Our Publishing Journey!

If you would like to receive FREE BOOKS, please visit **www.senseipublishing.com**. Join our newsletter by entering your email address in the pop-up box

Follow Sensei Paul David on Amazon

CLICK THE LOGO BELOW

FREE BONUS!!!
Experience Over 25 FREE Engaging Guided Meditations!

Prized Skills & Practices for Adults & Kids. Help Restore Deep-Sleep, Lower Stress, Improve Posture, Navigate Uncertainty & More.

Download the Free Insight Timer App and click the link below:
http://insig.ht/sensei_paul

About Sensei Publishing

Sensei Publishing commits itself to helping people of all ages transform into better versions of themselves by providing high-quality and research-based self-development books with an emphasis on mental health and guided meditations. Sensei Publishing offers well-written e-books, audiobooks, paperbacks and online courses that simplify complicated but practical topics in line with its mission to inspire people towards positive transformation.

It's a great day to be alive!

About the Author

I create simple & transformative eBooks & Guided Meditations for Adults & Children proven to help navigate uncertainty, solve niche problems & bring families closer together.

I'm a former finance project manager, private pilot, jiu-jitsu instructor, musician & former University of Toronto Fitness Trainer. I prefer a science-based approach to focus on these & other areas in my life to stay humble & hungry to evolve. I hope you enjoy my work and I'd love to hear your feedback.

- It's a great day to be alive!

Sensei Paul David

Scan & Follow/Like/Subscribe: Facebook, Instagram, YouTube: @senseipublishing

Scan using your phone/iPad camera for Social Media Visit us at www.senseipublishing.com and sign up for our newsletter to learn more about our exciting books and to experience our FREE Guided Meditations for Kids & Adults.

www.ingramcontent.com/pod-product-compliance
Lightning Source LLC
Chambersburg PA
CBHW072118070526
44585CB00016B/1488